THE CITY LIBRARY
SPRINGFIELD, (MA) CITY LIBRARY

Emily's
Place for
Children

DISCARDED BY
THE CITY LIBRARY

YouTube

Lisa Owings

An Imprint of Abdo Publishing
abdopublishing.com

abdopublishing.com

Published by Abdo Publishing, a division of ABDO, PO Box 398166, Minneapolis, Minnesota 55439. Copyright © 2017 by Abdo Consulting Group, Inc. International copyrights reserved in all countries. No part of this book may be reproduced in any form without written permission from the publisher. Checkerboard Library™ is a trademark and logo of Abdo Publishing.

Printed in the United States of America, North Mankato, Minnesota
062016
092016

THIS BOOK CONTAINS RECYCLED MATERIALS

Design: Emily Love, Mighty Media, Inc.
Production: Mighty Media, Inc.
Editor: Rebecca Felix
Cover Photos: Shutterstock
Interior Photos: Alamy, pp. 5, 6, 10, 11; AP Images, pp. 9, 17; Getty Images, pp. 15, 19, 21; iStockphoto, pp. 13, 27; Shutterstock, pp. 4, 7, 23, 25, 29

Publishers Cataloging-in-Publication Data
Names: Owings, Lisa, author.
Title: YouTube / by Lisa Owings.
Description: Minneapolis, MN : Abdo Publishing, [2017] | Series: Social media sensations | Includes index.
Identifiers: LCCN 2016934279 | ISBN 9781680781953 (lib. bdg.) | ISBN 9781680775808 (ebook)
Subjects: LCSH: YouTube (Firm)--Juvenile literature. | YouTube (Electronic resource)--Juvenile literature. | Online social networks--Juvenile literature. | Internet industry--Juvenile literature.
Classification: DDC 006.7--dc23
LC record available at /http://lccn.loc.gov/2016934279

Contents

	Social Media Profile	4
	Meet the Founders	5
Chapter 1	What Is YouTube?	6
Chapter 2	Successful Start-Up	8
Chapter 3	A Google Company	10
Chapter 4	YouTube Users	12
Chapter 5	Getting Famous	14
Chapter 6	Podcast Popularity	16
Chapter 7	A Bigger Picture	18
Chapter 8	Building Communities	20
Chapter 9	Staying Safe	22
Chapter 10	Staying on Top	24
	A Guide to YouTube	28
	Glossary	30
	Websites	31
	Index	32

SOCIAL MEDIA PROFILE

YouTube

URL: http://www.youtube.com

PURPOSE: YouTube is a video-sharing website. Users can watch, **upload**, and comment on videos.

CURRENT CEO: Susan Wojcicki

NUMBER OF USERS: More than 1 billion

* **MAY 2005**
  YouTube is launched

* **NOVEMBER 2006**
  Google buys YouTube

* **JULY 2010**
  Maximum length of videos increases to 15 minutes

* **DECEMBER 2011**
  YouTube introduces channels

Meet the Founders

STEVE CHEN was born in Taiwan. He moved to the United States at age 15. Later, Chen attended college at the University of Illinois at Urbana-Champaign. After graduation, he began working at the e-payment website PayPal.

CHAD HURLEY is from Pennsylvania. He earned a degree in fine art from the Indiana University of Pennsylvania. After graduation, Hurley also got a job at PayPal, where he met Chen.

JAWED KARIM was born in Germany. He moved to the United States around age 13. He went to college with Chen, but dropped out to work at PayPal. Chen, Hurley, and Karim left PayPal to start YouTube in 2005. Karim later left YouTube to continue in school.

CHAPTER 1

What Is YouTube?

A friend throws down some serious moves at the skate park. You film her with your phone and **upload** the video to YouTube. Overnight, the video goes **viral**. Your friend is a worldwide star! That's the power of YouTube.

YouTube is a video-sharing community. The site makes it easy for almost anyone to show videos to the world. YouTube plays host to all kinds of videos. Viewers can watch how-to videos, funny cat videos, and more. And for every person who

About one-third of all people on the Internet are YouTube users.

Singer PSY's "Gangnam Style" video has had more than 2 billion views on YouTube!

uploads a video, hundreds more have an opinion about it. Users are free to comment on videos and share them across the Internet.

CHAPTER 2

Successful Start-Up

Steve Chen, Chad Hurley, and Jawed Karim founded YouTube. They met while working for the e-payment website PayPal. There, they discussed many ideas for building their own Internet **start-up**. One idea became YouTube!

The first YouTube site went up in May 2005. It was meant to be a video dating service. But people **uploaded** all kinds of videos. The founders went with it.

YouTube videos could only be up to 10 minutes long. By 2006, these short videos were getting millions of views a day. And thousands of new videos were uploaded daily.

Despite their early successes, YouTube's founders also faced challenges. As traffic increased, YouTube's founders hired people to maintain the site. The trio sought investors to help pay the employees' salaries and other costs. They needed money to keep the site going.

Hurley (left) and Chen (right) met in 1999 and worked together for 15 years.

Additionally, many videos **violated** the creators' **copyrights**. The YouTube founders feared **lawsuits** could put them out of business. They knew something had to change.

CHAPTER 3

A Google Company

In November 2006, YouTube found a solution for its funding. That year, Internet search giant Google bought the site for $1.65 billion. Although it was owned by Google, YouTube ran independently and kept its workers. However, by 2010, all three founders had left YouTube.

When Google took over, YouTube quickly addressed the website's **copyright** issues. It did this by paying other companies for **permission** to use their content.

Google's headquarters is called the Googleplex. YouTube is one of many products worked on there.

This allowed YouTube users to post videos containing the content.

YouTube continued making changes. In July 2010, the video length limit increased to 15 minutes. And users could apply for **permission** to **upload** even longer videos. Many users began uploading movies and television shows.

In December 2011, YouTube introduced channels. Each channel features all videos posted by a single user. Channels are also organized by topic.

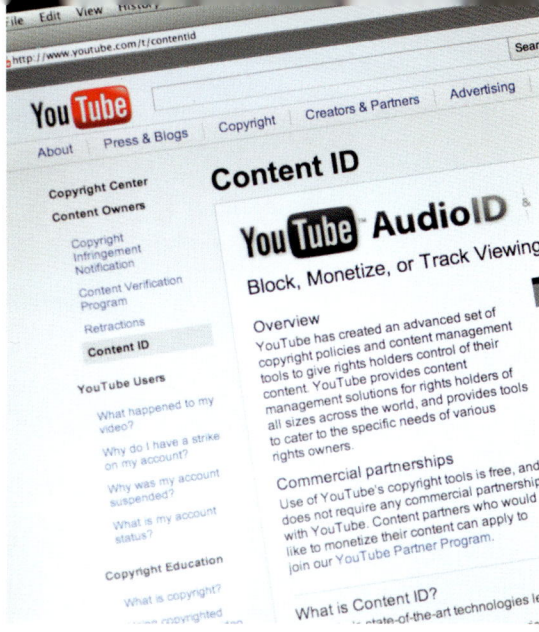

Content ID

Dealing with video **copyrights** is a huge job. To make it easier, YouTube created a system called Content ID. Copyright holders give YouTube copies of their files. YouTube keeps a database of millions of these files. Each new video is scanned against the database. If anything in the video matches anything in the database, YouTube's system may take the video down.

CHAPTER 4

YouTube Users

YouTube works hard to keep its users coming back to its site. As a result, YouTube is the most visited website after Google and Facebook. Most people visit to watch videos. Users can simply search for videos they want to watch. Or they can create an account and **subscribe** to channels. Logged-in users can also comment on, like, and dislike others' videos.

Of course, there wouldn't be videos without content creators. These are the people behind, or in front of, the cameras. Any YouTube account holder can **upload** videos. Video quality ranges

Did You Know?

YouTube's first content creator was co-founder Karim. His "Me at the Zoo" was the first video ever uploaded to the site. In it, Karim stands in front of elephants and talks about how cool their long trunks are.

Subscribers can receive emails from YouTube channels about new videos.

from quick smartphone clips to videos filmed using professional camera and lighting setups.

YouTube offers content creators tools to personalize their channels. These tools include a video-editing program and library of music for soundtracks. Creators can even **stream** live events on their channels. For example, they might stage a live question-and-answer session, where they respond to viewer comments.

Content creators can also partner with YouTube. These creators allow ads to play before their videos. In return, the creators get to share in YouTube's profits.

CHAPTER 5

Getting Famous

For most users, YouTube is just a fun hobby. However, if a content creator's videos attract enough viewers, his or her YouTube hobby can turn into a career. Some famous YouTubers are discovered through their **viral** videos.

Justin Bieber is one such success story. In 2008, a talent scout came across YouTube videos of Bieber singing. Soon the videos had thousands of views. Bieber kept posting, and people kept watching. Bieber became a pop star!

Many people have had great success as content creators. Some content creators that partner with YouTube make a living off the money they earn

Did You Know?

Several YouTube channels earn more than $100,000 a year from advertising!

Justin Bieber performing in 2009, shortly after becoming famous on YouTube

from the partnership. But that doesn't mean it's easy to become a professional YouTuber. There is plenty of competition! Creators need to have great content and good luck.

CHAPTER 6

Podcast Popularity

YouTube has made people into Internet stars. Many YouTube stars have turned this success into careers in television, film, and music. Some have also branched out into other digital platforms, such as podcasting.

A podcast is an audio or video recording. Podcasts can be listened to or viewed on iPods, smartphones, tablets, and computers. The first podcasts came out in 2005. These were sound recordings. They were like radio shows, but people could listen to them whenever they chose.

Today, there are video podcasts as well. They have given YouTube stars and other artists more opportunities to connect with fans. Many of these podcasts can be watched on YouTube.

One feature that has made podcasting popular is its **accessibility**. Nearly all podcasts are free, so anyone with the right device can **download** and listen to them.

YouTube star Jenna Marbles (right) hosts a popular podcast called "Jenna & Julien Podcast." On it, she and her boyfriend, Julien Solomita (left), often interview other YouTube stars.

Accessibility for creators has also helped make podcasting popular. Like YouTube videos, podcasts don't require a script, producer, or broadcast program. Anyone with the proper equipment can create one.

CHAPTER 7
A Bigger Picture

YouTube is not purely used for entertainment. Many people and companies also use YouTube videos to influence viewers. Companies post videos to sell their products. They buy ads to be played during users' videos.

Politicians post YouTube videos to try to convince viewers to support them. In 2007, videos posted by Barack Obama supporters helped him win the 2008 US presidential election. Obama was reelected in 2012 with the help of YouTube and its users' votes.

YouTube can also help create social awareness. The It Gets Better Project began with a 2010 video. It was made after many lesbian, gay, bisexual, and transgender (LGBT) youths took their own lives due to bullying. People in the video assure LGBT youth their lives will get better.

YouTube videos can also become a form of protest. In 2010, the **Arab Spring** protests began in the Middle East

President Barack Obama's YouTube channel has more than 500,000 subscribers.

against the region's governments. YouTubers shared videos of clashes between governments and protesters. These users also planned protests through YouTube. This helped **democracy** spread throughout the Middle East.

19

CHAPTER 8

Building Communities

YouTube offers many people a way to educate themselves. YouTubers post videos containing everything from college-level classes to how to fix a toilet. As viewers with similar interests watch the same videos, YouTube communities often develop. Users in these communities learn from and inspire one another. The drive to have the best, most popular videos keeps them improving.

YouTube can help people work together to create wonderful things. In 2011, the YouTube Symphony Orchestra formed. Musicians across the globe tried out by posting videos of themselves playing.

Did You Know?

The YouTube concert in Sydney had more than 30 million viewers. It was the biggest live-streaming event yet.

The best musicians were chosen to travel to Sydney, Australia. A week of practice ended in a concert at the Sydney Opera House. It was **streamed** live on YouTube. This is just one example of how YouTube brings people from all corners of the globe together.

The YouTube Symphony Orchestra consisted of 101 musicians.

CHAPTER 9

Staying Safe

Today, YouTube is one of the most popular ways to share ideas using videos. It is a great resource. However, **online** video sharing can also be unsafe. When sharing information online, YouTube users must take steps to do so safely.

When you make a YouTube video, your face may be in it. You may reveal things about your surroundings and age too. Be careful you don't reveal too much. Never give out information people could use to find you. This includes your full name, address, and phone number.

Once your video is online, other users might share it. You may not be able to control who sees it. Would you be okay with your parents or teachers seeing your video? If not, think again about posting it.

YouTube allows users to change the privacy settings on their videos. Videos set to unlisted can be seen only by

If others appear in a video you make, get their permission before uploading it to YouTube.

those with whom you share a video link. But those you share with can also share the video link. They may send it to others.

Cyberbullying can be another problem on YouTube. Anyone with an account can comment on videos. Some content creators receive many **negative** comments. If you become a target of cyberbullying, tell an adult you trust. Then report the bullying to YouTube.

CHAPTER 10

Staying on Top

YouTube has been a leader in **online** video for more than a decade. However, the company still faces many challenges, such as keeping popular users as content creators. **Copyright** issues continue to be a problem. YouTube takes measures to protect copyright, but as more and more users add content, the company struggles to obtain **permissions** fast enough.

YouTube executives know it's hard work to stay successful. They aim to keep improving the site. Part of that means making YouTube videos playable everywhere. At one time, YouTube videos only worked on computers. Now, users are able to watch videos on computers, tablets, smartphones, and more.

But having YouTube videos **available** on many devices doesn't matter if the videos won't actually play. **Buffering** is another challenge YouTube faces. Users can only

More than half of all YouTube views are done on smartphones or tablets.

watch content once it has fully **buffered**, or loaded. Older devices and poor Internet connectivity can create slow buffering. Videos that buffer too long can cause users to become frustrated and leave the site.

It's not clear whether YouTube will be able to get rid of buffering entirely. But the goal is for videos to be playable with the slowest connection on the oldest device.

Copyright and **technology** issues are not the only challenges for YouTube. The site must also keep users watching after they click on their first video link. To this end, the site tries to **predict** what types of videos users will want to see. It suggests videos related to the ones users have watched. Then, users can just keep clicking.

YouTube also offers apps. In November 2015, YouTube launched YouTube Music. This app allows users to search for songs, music videos, and artists. Unlike competitors' apps, YouTube Music also features live concert clips and videos on how to play certain songs.

YouTube Kids is another new app. It is a collection of kid-friendly videos. Parents can use the app to provide their children with an easy way to search kid-friendly content.

What are you looking for when you log onto YouTube? Chances are, you'll find it. And in case you don't, YouTube will keep offering new content in the future.

Did You Know?

Three hundred hours of video are uploaded to YouTube every minute!

Users can connect their YouTube accounts with other social media sites, such as Twitter.

But perhaps the most exciting aspect of YouTube's future is that you, the viewer, will help shape it. Whether you use YouTube to change the world or to show off your adorable cat is up to you. Whatever you decide, the rest of the world will be watching!

A GUIDE TO
YouTube

Anyone age 13 or older can have a YouTube account.

Only people with YouTube accounts can **upload** videos. But anyone can watch YouTube videos.

Users can sign up at YouTube's website. Or they can **download** the YouTube app to their smartphones or tablets.

To upload videos, users sign in to their YouTube accounts. Then they click "upload" and select the video files to be uploaded.

It can be fun to comment on others' videos. But users should be kind. It's important to remember there is a real person behind each username.

YouTube users should remove any rude comments their videos receive. If a user receives threatening comments, he or she should report the comments to YouTube.

If a user sees something scary or **inappropriate** in a YouTube video, he or she can report the content to YouTube.

Glossary

accessibility – the quality of being easy to have or use by many people.

Arab Spring – a series of protests leading to changes in government across North Africa and the Middle East.

available – able to be had or used.

buffer – to store or collect data while it is being transferred or processed.

copyright – the legal right to control the use of something created for a certain period of time.

cyberbully – to tease, hurt, or threaten someone online.

democracy – a governmental system in which the people vote on how to run their country.

download – to transfer data from a computer network to a single computer or device.

inappropriate – not right or suited for a purpose or situation.

lawsuit – a case held before a court.

negative – bad or hurtful.

online – connected to the Internet.

permission – formal consent.

predict – to guess something ahead of time on the basis of observation, experience, or reasoning.

start-up – a new company started by the people who will run it.

stream – to transfer data, such as video, in a steady stream so it can be watched or played immediately.

subscribe – to sign up to receive something on a regular basis.

technology – the science of how something works.

upload – to transfer data from a computer to a larger network.

violate – to break or ignore a law, rule, or basic right.

viral – quickly or widely spread, usually by electronic communication.

Websites

To learn more about Social Media Sensations, visit **booklinks.abdopublishing.com**. These links are routinely monitored and updated to provide the most current information available.

Index

A
advertising, 13, 18
Arab Spring, 18, 19

B
Bieber, Justin, 14
bullying, 18

C
celebrities, 14, 16
channels, 4, 11, 12
Chen, Steve, 5, 8
commenting, 4, 7, 12, 13
copyrights, 9, 10, 24, 26
cyberbullying, 23

F
Facebook, 12
fame, 6, 14, 15, 16

G
Germany, 5
Google, 4, 10, 12

H
Hurley, Chad, 5, 8, 9, 10

I
Indiana University of Pennsylvania, 5
investors, 8
It Gets Better Project, 18

K
Karim, Jawed, 5, 8, 9, 10

L
lawsuits, 9
lesbian, gay, bisexual, transgender (LGBT), 18

M
Middle East, 18, 19
mobile devices, 6, 13, 16, 24, 25

O
Obama, Barack, 18
online safety, 22, 23

P
PayPal, 5, 8
Pennsylvania, 5
podcasts, 16, 17
presidential election, US, 18
privacy, 22, 23

S
skate parks, 6
social awareness, 18
streaming, 13, 21
Sydney Opera House, 21
Sydney, Australia, 21

T
Taiwan, 5

U
United States, 5
University of Illinois at Urbana-Champaign, 5

V
video buffering, 24, 25
video dating, 8
video editing, 13
video length, 8, 11

W
Wojcicki, Susan, 4

Y
YouTube Kids, 26
YouTube Music, 26
YouTube Symphony Orchestra, 20, 21